MASTERING ART
PAINTING

Anthony Hodge

CONTENTS

© Archon Press Ltd 2003

Produced by
Archon Press Ltd
28 Percy Street
London W1T 2BZ

New edition first published in Great Britain in 2003 by
Franklin Watts
96 Leonard Street
London EC2A 4XD

Original edition published as
Hands on Arts and Crafts – Painting

ISBN: 0–7496–4959–3

Design: Phil Kay
Editors: Nicola Cameron, Jen Green
Paintings: Anthony Hodge
Illustrations: Ron Hayward Associates

Printed in UAE

Introduction

"An artist is not a special kind of person, but every person is a special kind of artist."

A. Coomaraswamy, writer and artist.

This book provides an introduction to a series of ideas and techniques that will help you express yourself with paint. Painting is an area in which everyone can be of equal value, because each person's work is unique. Some will have an eye for detail; others form an impression of the world. These differences will be reflected in how you paint.

Freedom to experiment

The projects in this book cover a wide range of painting. We will start with tools and materials, colour-mixing and practical skills. Later, a series of projects will introduce ways of using these techniques, as well as using your own ideas.

What you need

You will need to wear old clothes which may get splashed with paint. You will also need newspaper or an old sheet to cover the surface on which you work, and somewhere to put your work while it dries. If you use oil paint, you will need white spirit and rags, followed by soap and water, to clean your brushes.

▲ "Here is a detail from a seascape that I painted at Newlyn Harbour in Cornwall. Even when you paint from life, it's important to feel free to experiment and bring in ideas from your imagination.

If an impulse comes to you, go along with it and see where it leads you. Some of the best ideas can come to you when you are least expecting them. So, keep an open mind, relax and above all, be sure to enjoy yourself."

Tools and Materials

Most paint is applied with brushes, but there are many other ways paint can be applied. Make a collection of some brushes and other mark-making implements such as sponges and sticks, and get ready for an experiment session with them.

A good palette is an important tool to mix your colours on. It must be large enough to hold plenty of paint, and have room left over for extra colour mixing. A wooden palette from an art shop is good as it is seasoned wood and can be cleaned easily. Otherwise, plastic or any other non-absorbent surface will do.

Poster paint is a cheap form of gouache. It comes in pots or paint boxes. Make sure you get plenty of colour on your brushes.

Which paint suits you best?

Colours are made of pigments (coloured powders), most of which are mined from the ground and mixed with binding materials to perform different jobs. You may find one kind of paint suits you so well that you use it all the time, or you may like a change from one to another. Other kinds of paints not shown here are emulsion, tempera and gloss.

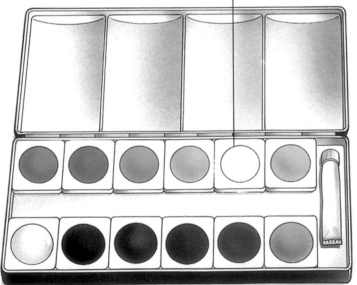

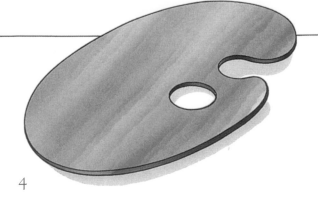

Acrylic is a paint made of plastic. It can be used thin like watercolour or thick like oil. It dries quickly, so don't squeeze out too much.

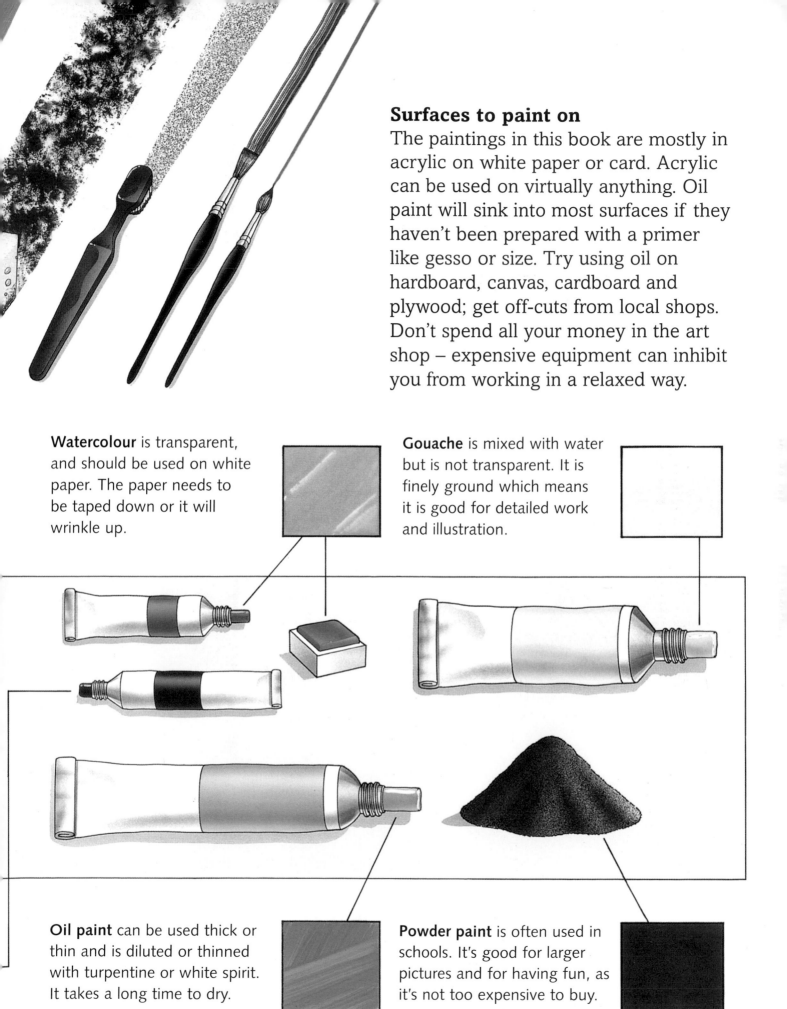

Surfaces to paint on

The paintings in this book are mostly in acrylic on white paper or card. Acrylic can be used on virtually anything. Oil paint will sink into most surfaces if they haven't been prepared with a primer like gesso or size. Try using oil on hardboard, canvas, cardboard and plywood; get off-cuts from local shops. Don't spend all your money in the art shop – expensive equipment can inhibit you from working in a relaxed way.

Watercolour is transparent, and should be used on white paper. The paper needs to be taped down or it will wrinkle up.

Gouache is mixed with water but is not transparent. It is finely ground which means it is good for detailed work and illustration.

Oil paint can be used thick or thin and is diluted or thinned with turpentine or white spirit. It takes a long time to dry.

Powder paint is often used in schools. It's good for larger pictures and for having fun, as it's not too expensive to buy.

Feeling Your Way

An important part of painting is enjoying using the materials. This project shows what the materials can do rather than what you can do. Just watch what happens and don't be too critical of yourself.

You will need a large piece of paper and the paints, brushes and mark-making tools you gathered earlier.

An exercise in mark-making

This project is about making different kinds of marks. With different tools you can make blobs, smears, draggings, squidges, anything. Try using different types of paintbrushes, thick and thin, your fingers, a palette knife and even a toothbrush.

On your marks

The marks you make will sometimes accidentally look like real things. Some tools are good for creating leaves, others for clouds and so on. The marks in these examples look like foliage, grass and flowers. Cover a page with different marks, pick out the ones which remind you of real things and then make them part of a separate painting of your own using appropriate colours.

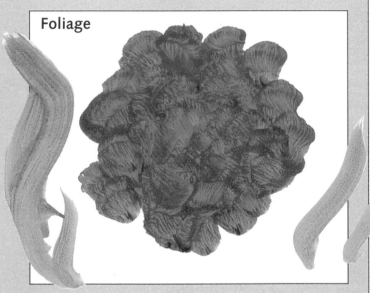

Foliage

Grass

Flowers

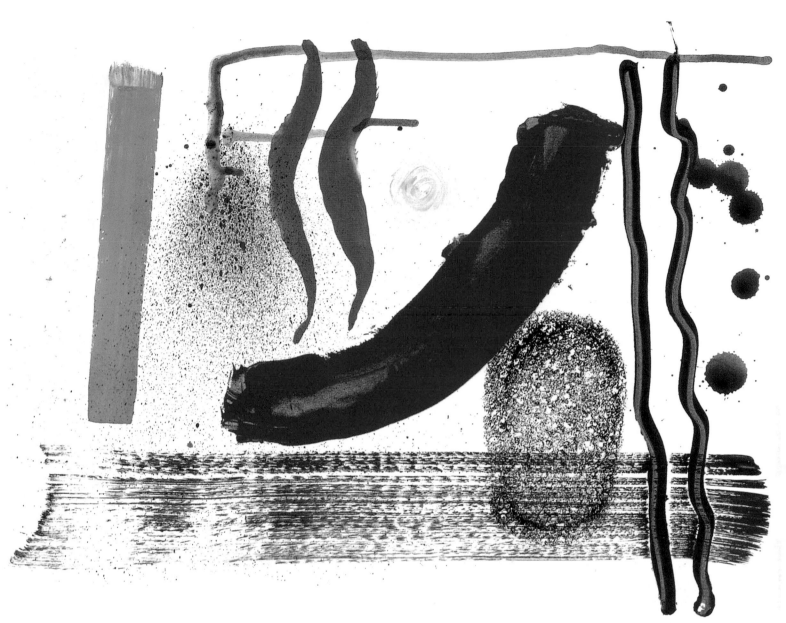

▲ *"Above is a variety of marks I made using colours at random and as many different tools as I could find. Try and work out yourself which tools have created each mark. After you have experimented with this, choose colours to suit particular kinds of marks, or try the whole project in one colour."*

Slow or speedy?

The kind of paint used here is acrylic, but use whatever you have or try several kinds of paint together. Don't try and make a 'proper' picture but concentrate on the different effects you can produce. At this stage the marks don't 'mean' anything, but some may look speedy and others slow. Some are soft, others look rough. See how different tools, for example, a soft brush or a hard palette knife, make the paint behave in very different ways. Also, try thinning your paints.

7

Pure Colour

This project is to give you a chance to get to know the colours in your paintbox and to practise using them in their pure form, without mixing them together.

If you look around you, you will see all kinds of colours, some bright, some dull, some easy to name, and some not so. Some painters avoid looking at real things and just make things up! Others like to paint what they see, at least from time to time.

Choosing your subject

Make a collection of objects that correspond as closely as possible with the six pure colours from the colour wheel (bottom right). Find something red, blue, green, yellow, orange and purple. You should also include a background – a bright curtain or coloured paper. Arrange your objects in a group so that you can see them clearly and they aren't in each other's way. Try to match the colours to your subjects.

You may like the bright colours so much that in future you may paint things brighter than they really are.

Keep the colours clean when painting by using a clean brush for each new colour.

▼ *"For the painting below I made a simple drawing in pencil. I spent some time deciding where the colours would go. You can see that some of the marks look a bit like the ones I made on the previous page. Try this yourself and choose the one you like best."*

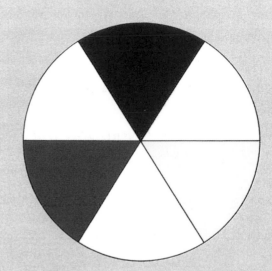

Primary colours

Here are the three primary colours and their position on the 'colour wheel'. There are many kinds of reds, yellows and blues but the primaries are the purest colours.

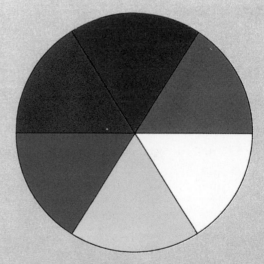

Secondary colours

Here are the primaries with their neighbours, orange, green and purple. These are the secondary colours, mixed from the two primaries on either side. Try painting the colour wheel yourself.

Mixing Colours

The pure colours used on the previous page can be put into opposite pairs or complementaries. These are red and green, yellow and purple, and blue and orange. Black and white are also opposites. Some pictures are painted with two complementaries, creating other colours by mixing them in different ways. Landscapes are often made of red and green, and these are the two colours used in the picture opposite, mixed with white in places.

Landscapes in pairs of colours

In autumn when the sky is often clear and the leaves are bright, or in spring with new life growing, other pairs of colours may be more appropriate. Winter could be seen as black and white. See if you can think of other subjects which would suit a particular pair of complementaries. Every colour, however subtle, has its own complementary.

Paint a simple landscape in a pair of complementaries mixed with white. You will find that you don't need many colours to paint an interesting and atmospheric picture. Use different kinds of brushwork, thick and thin, fast and slow, for different effects.

Inside or out?

If you enjoy painting from life, go out looking for a subject or just paint the view from your window. Or you may prefer painting a place you know from memory, or just making something up. Begin painting by mixing some colours on the palette, keeping them fresh and separate.

▶ *"In the painting on the right I have used pure colour in the foreground (the part of the picture which looks nearest to the viewer), and mixes of red and green for the foliage and tree trunks beyond. For the sky, road and the grass in the distance I have added white. I made a pencil sketch first, then mixed my colours and began."*

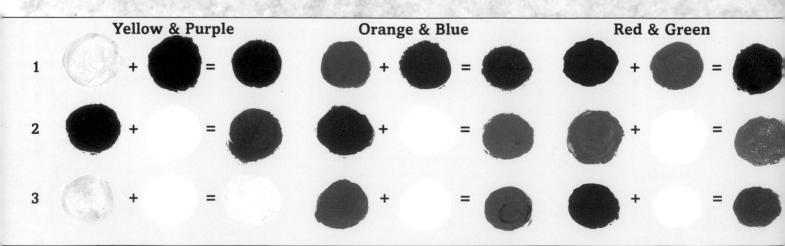

Pairs of opposites

Painted side by side, opposite colours enhance, or bring out, the best in each other. When mixed together they make interesting combinations. Colours mixed with white become more subtle. If pairs of opposites with white added are mixed together they make shades of grey.

White has the effect of making colours both lighter and less bright, with the exception of watercolours. With watercolour, subtlety is obtained by using varying amounts of water to dilute the colour. When you surround white with a pure colour, it will appear to be tinged with the complementary of the pure colour. Try it and see.

Brightness, Tone and Hue

Learning about colours is a bit like learning to speak a different language. If the first few pages of this book seem like hard work, think of them as teaching you a new vocabulary so that you can express yourself with confidence in future.

All colours have three qualities. These qualities are brightness, tone and hue. The brightness or dullness of a colour compares with a loud or soft note in music. Tone means how light or dark a colour is. A note in music has an equivalent high or low sound. Lastly, each colour also has a hue, which is equivalent to the actual note in music. The hue is the actual colour you are left with when differences in tone and brightness have been removed.

Seeing hue

The idea of this project is to make a picture in which all the colours are the same tone and as far as possible the same brightness. What you will then see is their hue. First choose and mix your colours. Look at them on the palette and change them around until they are the same tone. Use black to darken or quieten colours if they look too light or too bright. Keep the colours clean and flat. Arrange your composition. If colours of the same tone and brightness are placed side by side, (below), they seem to shimmer and dance together in front of your eyes.

Playing scales in colour

Brightness, tone and hue are illustrated in the colour scales below. The top one – brightness – demonstrates a progression of brightness to dullness, the middle – tone – shows light to dark tones, and the bottom one – hue – is a progression of the colour pink to green in the same tone and brightness, to demonstrate hue. Black is introduced here as a way to make colours darker in tone and less bright.

Brightness

Tone

Hue

◀ *"To keep colours on separate brushes clean, I stand the brushes bristles up in a tin with holes punched in the lid. Alternatively, you could use a container filled with scrunched-up chicken wire."*

Black can also be used as a colour in its own right. Like white, it may appear to be affected by colours that surround it. Sometimes painters use lines of black to separate the colours in their pictures, like a stained glass window. This can bring order to a chaotic image.

Making It Look 'Real'

There is always a special kind of thrill in making something you paint look real. If you are painting an apple, how can you make it look solid, fresh and good enough to eat?

One way to make your pictures look real is to examine how light falls on the subject. As the sun moves across the sky and the shadows come and go, the appearance of your subject can change very much. The world changes constantly in front of you as you try to capture it, especially outside on a sunny day.

Careful observation

Find a simply coloured object, an apple or an orange perhaps. Look at how its hues, tones and brightness change as you move it around. Get to know the apple in all lights, and familiarise yourself with its shape and colours. Try placing the apple so that the light comes strongly from one direction. Paint the apple in your mind's eye before you begin. Then make three paintings, each showing a different effect of light and shadow. The light should be shown from the front, from the side and from the back.

Light is from the front

Light is from the side

14

Painting in 3-D

Some painters feel that the shadow of an object can be represented by the complementary of the colour that is in the light. Try different colours for the image and shadows to give the maximum 3-D effect.

▼ *"My examples below show the same apple in three different lights. The colours become gradually darker and more blue as the shadows deepen. Make your picture life-size or larger, so you can really show what's happening without focussing on smaller details."*

Light is from the back

Changing light

The diagrams above show the effects of light shone on a round form from different directions. Reproducing this effect involves blending colours. As the light changes to shadow, the colours change accordingly. Practise these changes on a separate piece of paper before beginning your painting.

Portraits

"Why can't you be more like an apple!" Cézanne used to shout at people he was painting. A head may be a bit like an apple but it has expressions and doesn't find it easy to stay still and always look the same.

Beginning work

The project here is to paint a portrait. Ask someone to pose for you who won't mind whether your picture is exactly like them or not. Make sure that your subject is comfortable and relaxed.

Step by step

Take time to have a good look at your subject. In pencil (1), and then with very thin paint (2), draw the simple shape of the face. Mark in the lines for the features as shown in the diagram below. Lightly draw in

the eyes, ears, nose, mouth and hair. Look closely at the colour of the skin, hair, clothes, and the background.

Setting the mood

Mix up the main colours you need. They, as much as anything else, will give the picture its mood. When you are satisfied with your ingredients, paint them down as flat areas of colour (3). Give your portrait depth and solidity by modelling highlights and shadows over the flat colours (4).

▶ *"My examples show the four stages described above. Light is shining on the face from one side, and I have introduced light and shadow areas accordingly. Don't be afraid of changing your picture as you go along. The character of your subject may only become clear gradually. It's important not to put in too many details at an early stage, as you may be reluctant to paint over them even if you should."*

Proportions of the head

The drawing near right shows the average proportions of the head. One thing that may surprise you is that the eyes are halfway down the head and not higher up. The lower part is divided in half again where the nose ends, and in half again at the mouth. The second picture shows the same head in *profile*, from a side view.

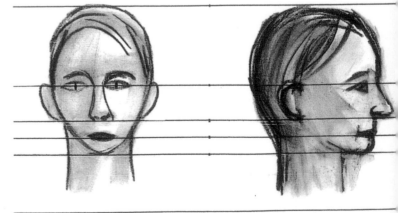

1

2

3

4

Mood and Feeling

This page is all about expressing feeling with paint. Imagine that you meet with an alien from outer space on a visit to Earth. This creature comes from a scientifically advanced planet whose inhabitants are incapable of experiencing emotion. Your paintings must express these unknown things to him/her/it.

Making the unseen visible

Painting, like music, has the power to communicate happiness, sadness, calm, rage. Decide what emotion you want to try first; it will help if you get in the mood yourself, perhaps by playing some appropriate music.

▲ Happiness

▼ Excitement

Be a conductor of energy

Let the emotion you have chosen wash over you. What colours and shapes come to mind? There isn't a right or wrong way of doing this. When you have finished, try a different emotion, sadness or boredom perhaps. If you ever say you feel bored, now is the time to paint the most boring picture you can!

◄▲ *"My paintings show two contrasting sets of emotions. Here are some pairs of adjectives you might like to try: angry and calm; relaxed and uncomfortable; friendly and hostile; extravagant and mean. Dream up other pairs yourself."*

▲ Misery

▲ Peacefulness

Mood, shape and colour

There are no strict rules linking colours with particular feelings. Blue is usually thought of as sad but it can also be peaceful; orange can be cheerful but also angry. Yellow can be warm like the sun. Shapes also express mood and emotion. A triangle sitting firmly on the ground might convey stability, or hope. A rectangle may seem calm or restrictive. A circle seems likely to move or float and might convey a sense of wholeness or isolation. A star might seem to explode with vitality. Which colours fit best with each of these shapes?

Expressing Yourself

Painters paint self-portraits for all kinds of reasons, but the most obvious has to be that your own face is always there when you want it. Have a good look in the mirror and see the shape of your face. Is it round, oval, square or heart-shaped? Ask yourself what kind of person you are. Are you cheerful or sad? Do you shout a lot or are you quiet? Do you like to do things quickly, or do you take your time? Using some of the ideas from the previous projects, try to combine careful observation and the expression of feeling in a portrait of yourself.

Getting started

Place your paper or board on an easel or rest it against a wall or the back of a chair in front of a mirror. Position yourself so that you can look at your painting without moving your head too much. Make a sketch as you did earlier, establishing the proportions of your face. Mix your colours until you are satisfied that they represent you.

Showing how you feel

Do several pictures of yourself in different moods and change the colours and the way you put on the paint accordingly. After the first painting, you may want to dispense with the mirror and paint your 'inner self' from imagination.

▲ *"These three portraits use colour to convey mood. This boy in shades of pink looks gentle and thoughtful."*

Features and expressions

Here are examples of the same face with three very different expressions, looking angry, frightened and perplexed. These emotions are conveyed through the shape of the mouth and eyes. Notice, however, that the eyebrows, hair, even the nose and ears also express emotion. Lines and shapes turning upwards look cheerful and full of life; turning down they look sad or fierce. To show perplexity the lines may turn in both directions.

▲ "I have tried to convey the scruffiness and good humour of this boy through the use of bright colours and jagged strokes.

▲ "My third sitter seemed anxious and sad. I chose gloomy colours and applied them with nervous, scratchy strokes."

Imagination

Imagination means image-making. With it you can create pictures of things that in real life could never happen (or not very often anyway). Through painting you can create a world which is strange, magical, shocking or just plain daft.

Unusual combinations

When two unrelated subjects come together in a painting, they can make something entirely new. The illustration near right shows a man and a tree. In the painting opposite, the same words came together to make a tree-man. If you look in the background you will see a man-tree.

Seeing pictures in your head

One way of getting ideas for a painting of this kind is to write down lots of ideas when you have them. Keep them on separate pieces of paper in a bag.

Pick pairs of them at random out of the bag. When you see two words together, what picture, if any, comes into your mind of how they could be joined? Practise seeing as much detail as possible in your mind's eye before starting to paint.

▶ *"My tree-man picture is painted with a big brush for the trees and sky and a smaller one for the head and hands. The brush marks in the foreground and in the foliage look like grass and leaves."*

Changing step by step

The idea of putting together two things and making a third can be a starting point for all kinds of ideas. Opposite you can see how a man changing into a tiger might work step by step. This process is called transformation or metamorphosis. Perhaps you can imagine how a similar sequence happened while the man was changing into a tree, which the main picture shows halfway through. There are many other ways of using your imagination. Dreams can provide images that can become powerful paintings – can you remember any of yours?

Composition

Composition means putting things together. If you taste the ingredients for a cake one by one, it is not the same as tasting the cake itself. In the same way your picture is made up of different ingredients that come together. Within it, coloured shapes and light and dark areas have to work together so that the picture can be seen as a whole.

Have a go yourself

A good way to practise composition is to make a collage. Tear coloured paper into the shapes you want and move them around to make a sense of unity before you glue them down.

Ripping off ideas

A good subject for this technique is people in action. Look through newspapers or magazines to find an image that you like. Then compose your own collage based loosely on the photograph. Don't glue anything down until you have tried your ingredients in a number of different positions first.

▶ *"My composition is triangular. Your eyes go up to the ball as the footballers do. The coloured bits for the arms and legs don't look very real on their own, but they play their part in the whole."*

An exciting journey

Compositions are often based on shapes like a triangle or a circle. Let your eyes follow the movement of the composition. In the team picture your eyes can either look along the rows of heads or move in a zigzag between them. In the hop, skip and jump picture below, look at the shapes and the movement of the action figures.

Perspective

Perspective, which means 'looking through', is a way of creating the illusion of three-dimensional space on the flat surface of a picture. Perspective gives the illusion of depth and distance to a picture, and the impression that we are looking through a window.

Getting angles right

It can sometimes be difficult to get a particular angle of a building or table exactly right, to show the perspective. Don't give up the idea of being good at art if you find this technique difficult to master. There are many other aspects of painting which you can still enjoy.

Background

Middle ground

Foreground

Creating distance

There are at least four different ways of showing that one thing is behind or in front of another (showing perspective). Many pictures combine several, though some use none at all.

For the painter, perhaps the most appropriate way of portraying distance is with colour.

◄ *"The sky in my picture opposite shows that a strong blue can appear to be in front of a paler, thinner blue as it fades towards the horizon. I vigorously applied the brightest colours in the foreground and middle distance."*

Darker colours tend to go back, or recede, in space. Light and bright ones tend to come forward. Think of how the rays of a yellow sun reach out from a background of blue sky.

The strongest contrasts in tone should be in the foreground. Colours in a landscape seem to get bluer and more misty the further away they are, and the same effect can be achieved in painting. Recession can also be emphasised by using thinner paint in the middle and in the background. Paint a landscape and test out these theories.

A sense of space

The first diagram is an example of 'linear' or line perspective. Lines that run parallel in the real world appear to meet at a point on the horizon called the 'vanishing point'. The second diagram shows an example of overlapping. The hill that blocks out part of another hill must be in front of it; the figure blocks them all out and is closest to you. In the third diagram, the darker and stronger lines and tones in the foreground appear to be in front of the softer, 'slower' lines.

Linear

Overlapping

Tonal

Different Ways of Seeing

Long ago, ancient civilisations had different ways of viewing the world than we in the West are familiar with today. Persian, Indian, Egyptian and Chinese cultures all evolved artistic traditions which reflected their own outlooks. The idea was to represent a scene showing many viewpoints at the same time.

Seeing the world as flat

Many modern painters have placed a similar importance on the picture as a flat pattern in which every part is of equal value. In their work, colours and shapes sit side by side on the surface of the picture, as they do in the main painting below, rather than trying to fool the eye and create the illusion of space.

Seeing from many angles

Try this approach with a painting of your own room at home. This project is not about standing on one spot, and painting what you see with a mathematical precision. Walk around your room and decide which viewpoint is best for each of the objects you want to include. You could also put yourself in the picture.

▲ *"Above is a picture I painted from a single viewpoint with linear perspective. The space is defined by receding lines which make the front look bigger and the rear smaller."*

▶ *"This painting involves different viewpoints. The tabletop is seen from above, the vase from the side, while the fruit bowl is a bit of both."*

28

Through Egyptian eyes

A striking example of multi-viewpoint seeing is found in the art of the ancient Egyptians, whose style of painting remained almost unchanged for 5,000 years. Egyptian artistic tradition represented things from particular angles, regardless of whether it was possible to see these angles in the real world. Artists felt that this method would best express the essence of their subject. For example, a face was shown from the side, but an eye was shown from the front.

29

Presentation

Your pictures will always look better when they are put into a mount or a frame and hung on a wall. Looking at your work over a period of time when it is exhibited will also help you to see it properly.

Reworking

You may notice some things in your picture that you want to change. You may find that there are parts that you don't like. A colour may appear too bright or too dull. Reworking should be approached with caution. If your picture is free and spontaneous, you may spoil it by overpainting.

When to stop

Judging the right moment to stop is an important skill to develop. When that decision is made, the painting has reached the end of its journey.

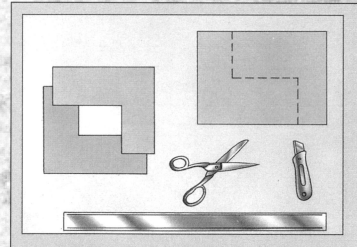

Selecting your image

If your painting does not seem to work satisfactorily as it is, a part of it may. Selecting which part to use can be fascinating. By cutting out a pair of L-shapes (above) and moving them over the picture, you can isolate one part of it, changing the size and shape of your composition very easily. When you are happy with it, measure your 'new' painting for the dimensions of your mount.

Mounting your work

Mounts should be cut equally on both sides. Be sure your mount is wider at the bottom than at the top, as shown in the middle mount below. Otherwise when it is hanging, the mount will look unbalanced. A pale grey or cream mount is right for many pictures, but sometimes coloured mounts are effective. Choose a colour which brings out the mood or the colours of the picture. On the whole, avoid very brightly coloured mounts, as they can draw attention away from your painting.

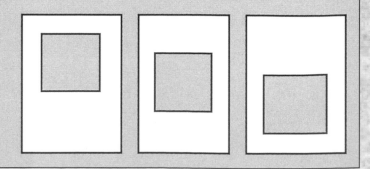

Practical Tips

Your starting kit
Whichever **paint** you choose, you will need at least five colours – try cadmium red, cadmium yellow, ultramarine (blue), white and black. Add yellow ochre, viridian (green), burnt umber and cobalt blue if you can.

Many kinds of **brushes** are available, suitable for different sorts of paint. You will need at least three brushes to begin with: a thick and a thin coarse brush, and a fine brush for details. Brush prices vary greatly; more expensive ones will probably last longer and create better results.

A **palette knife** can be used to apply oil or acrylic paint, to produce hard, flat marks or to build up layers of paint. For a **palette,** you could use an old plate or tin lid. You will need water and some small containers for thinners.

Preparing your surface
Before you use oil or acrylic paint, you will need to **prime** your surface, unless you are using a prepared canvas. For acrylic paint, use an acrylic primer. For oil paint, give your surface a coat of primer such as size or gesso.

Stretching your paper
Stretching your paper may be necessary if you use water-soluble paint. Wet the paper in water. Place it on a board, and smooth out the creases with a sponge. Tape it to the board with brown paper tape, and let it dry.

Adding thinners
Paint is usually thinned or diluted. Watercolours, gouache, powder and poster paint are diluted with water. Oil paint is thinned with linseed oil and turpentine or white spirit. To give different effects, acrylic paint can be diluted with various liquids.

Cleaning up
After using water-soluble paints, brushes should be rinsed in water immediately and stood up to dry. After using oils, brushes should be wiped with a rag, cleaned with white spirit and then with soap and water. Put your oil painting somewhere safe to dry – it may take a few months. You can then coat it with varnish.

Index